THE MOON

by Thomas K. Adamson

raintree
a Capstone company — publishers for children

Raintree is an imprint of Capstone Global Library Limited, a company incorporated in England and Wales having its registered office at 264 Banbury Road, Oxford, OX2 7DY – Registered company number: 6695582

www.raintree.co.uk
myorders@raintree.co.uk

Edited by Alison Deering
Designed by Sarah Bennett
Original illustrations © Capstone Global Library Limited 2023
Picture research by Julie De Adder and Svetlana Zhurkin
Production by Katy LaVigne
Originated by Capstone Global Library Ltd

978 1 3982 4794 9 (hardback)
978 1 3982 4798 7 (paperback)

British Library Cataloguing in Publication Data
A full catalogue record for this book is available from the British Library.

Acknowledgements
We would like to thank the following for permission to reproduce photographs: Shutterstock: 3000ad, 4–5, AstroStar, 16, BlueRingMedia, 19, flashpict, 11, kaopanom, 15, Mike Pellinni, cover, pullia, 17, sdecoret, 9, SunflowerMomma, 18, Thitiwat Luechaudompan, 1, Tim Murphy, 6, Tom Reichner, 8, tomasandrascik, 10, Triff, 4 (top left) and throughout, udaix, 7, Viktor Klagyivik, 12–13; Svetlana Zhurkin: 20, 21

Every effort has been made to contact copyright holders of material reproduced in this book. Any omissions will be rectified in subsequent printings if notice is given to the publisher.

Printed and bound in India.

Contents

Words in **bold** are in the glossary.

What are moons?

Moons are natural objects that move around **planets**. Earth has one moon. It is the brightest object in our sky other than the Sun.

The Moon is not always the same distance from Earth. On average, it is 384,400 km (238,855 miles) away. That is about 30 Earths!

Why does the Moon rise in one place and set in another?

The Earth spins. That is what makes the Moon rise and set. Because Earth rotates to the east, the Moon moves across the sky from east to west.

 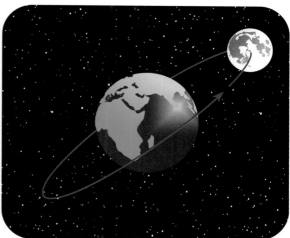

The Moon also moves around the Earth. It moves in the same direction that the Earth spins. The Moon gets ahead of the Earth's rotation. That's why it rises about 50 minutes later each day.

Why does the Moon change shape?

The Moon itself doesn't change shape. But our view of the Moon does change!

The Moon does not make its own light. Sunlight bounces off the Moon's surface, lighting up half of it. The other half is dark.

As the Moon moves around Earth, how much of that bright side we see changes. We see this as the changing **phases** of the Moon.

What are the phases of the Moon?

There are eight phases of the Moon. During a **new moon**, the far side of the Moon is lit. We can't see it from Earth.

A **crescent** moon is a curved sliver. A quarter moon looks like a semicircle. The moon looks brighter during the **gibbous** phase.

PHASES OF THE MOON

new moon

crescent moon

quarter moon

gibbous moon

full moon

gibbous moon

quarter moon

crescent moon

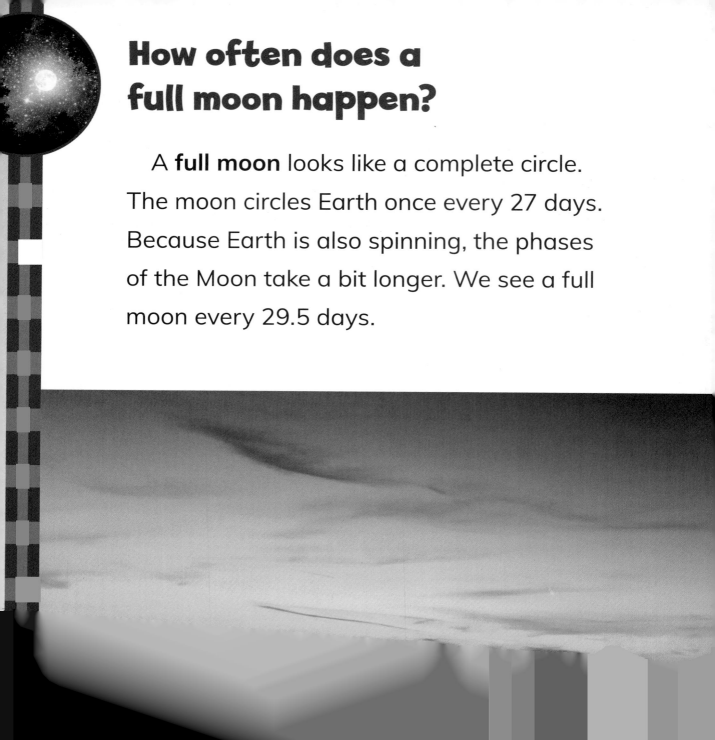

How often does a full moon happen?

A **full moon** looks like a complete circle. The moon circles Earth once every 27 days. Because Earth is also spinning, the phases of the Moon take a bit longer. We see a full moon every 29.5 days.

Can we see the Moon during the day?

Yes! But we might not notice it. A bright blue sky makes the Moon hard to spot. It's easier to see the bright Moon shining against the black night sky.

There is never a full moon in the daytime sky. The Moon and Sun are on opposite sides of Earth during a full moon.

Does the Moon disappear?

No! But sometimes it looks like it. An **eclipse** happens when Earth's shadow covers the Moon. During a total eclipse, the Moon is completely covered.

In a partial eclipse, only part of the shadow lands on the Moon. The shadow gradually grows. Then it goes away without completely covering the Moon.

Does the Moon affect us?

The Moon is far away. But its **gravity** pulls on Earth. It changes Earth's shape!

We notice this change most easily as **tides** along ocean beaches. Tides are the rising and falling of ocean levels caused by the Moon.

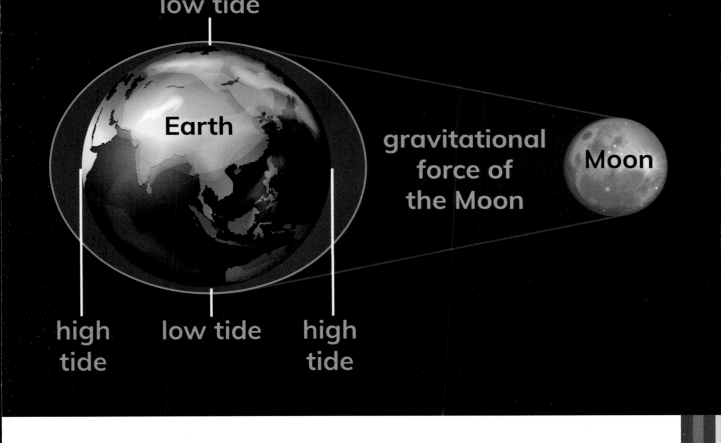

The Moon's gravity pulls on the closest side of Earth. It also pulls on the side furthest away. That causes high tide. Low tide occurs on the other parts of Earth as it rotates.

Make sweet moon phases

Use sandwich biscuits to make the different phases of the Moon!

What you need

- 4–8 round sandwich biscuits

- toothpick

- butter knife

What to do

1. Carefully remove one side of the biscuit.

2. Use the toothpick to draw the shape of one moon phase in the filling.

3. Use the butter knife to lift part of the filling off the biscuit. This empty part represents the dark side of the Moon. The filling that's left represents the bright part of the Moon that we see.

4. Create the rest of the moon phases with the other biscuits.

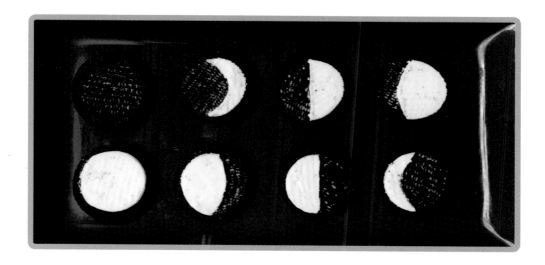

Glossary

crescent curved shape that is wider in the middle than at the ends

eclipse event in which Earth's shadow passes over the Moon or the Moon's shadow passes over Earth

full moon Moon when it appears as a bright circle

gibbous when the lit part of the Moon looks larger than a semicircle and smaller than a full circle

gravity force that pulls objects together

moon object that moves around a planet

new moon phase of the Moon when its dark side is towards Earth

phase stage; the Moon's phases are the shapes that it appears to take over a month

planet large object that moves around a star; Earth is a planet

tide daily rising and falling of the ocean level

Find out more

Books

The Moon and Other Satellites (Our Place in the Universe), Ellen Labrecque (Raintree, 2020)

Night Sky and Day Sky (Engage Literacy), Anne Giulieri (Raintree, 2020)

The Usborne Book of the Moon, Laura Cowan (Usborne Publishing, 2019)

Websites

www.bbc.co.uk/bitesize/topics/zkbbkqt/articles/z3b3ydm
Learn more about the Moon.

www.dkfindout.com/uk/space/moon-landings
Find out about the Moon landings.

Index

About the author

Thomas K. Adamson has written lots of non-fiction books for kids. Sport, maths, science, cool vehicles – a bit of everything! When not writing, he likes to hike, watch films, eat pizza and, of course, read.
Tom lives in South Dakota, USA, with his wife, two sons and a Morkie called Moe.